This Business Journal Belongs To:

_____

Suppliers LIST

PRODUCT:	DESCRIPTION:	COMPANY/VENDOR:	WEBSITE URL:

Supply INVENTORY

PRODUCT:	SUPPLIER:	QTY:	COST:

Monthly SALES

DATE:	SOURCE	PRICE:	PROFIT:

Monthly INCOME TRACKER

MONTH: **YEAR:**

DATE:	DESCRIPTION:	GROSS:	NET:

Monthly EXPENSES

MONTH: **YEAR:**

DATE: **DESCRIPTION:**   **INVOICE #:**   **AMOUNT:**

Monthly BUDGET

MONTH: _____ **YEAR:** _____

OVERVIEW:	BUDGETED:	ACTUAL COST:
INCOME:		
EXPENSES:		
SAVINGS:		
OTHER:		

EXPENSE TRACKER

SUMMARY:	BUDGETED:	ACTUAL COST:	NOTES:

Product INVENTORY

PRODUCT:	DESCRIPTION:	QTY:	COST:

Mileage TRACKER

PERIOD OF:

DATE:	TO:	FROM:	PURPOSE:	TOTAL DISTANCE

Product PRICING

ITEM:	SUPPLY COST:	LABOR:	SHIPPING COST:	PROFIT:

Tax DEDUCTIONS

MONTH: _____   **YEAR:** _____

DATE:	DESCRIPTION:	AMOUNT:	NOTES:

Discount TRACKER

MONTH: **YEAR:**

ITEM: **DESCRIPTION:**   **REG PRICE:**   **SALE PRICE:**

Shipping TRACKER

ORDER #:	PRODUCT DESCRIPTION:	SHIP DATE:	TRACKING #:	SHIPPED:

Supplier CONTACTS

NAME	NAME
BUSINESS	BUSINESS
WEBSITE:	WEBSITE:
EMAIL:	EMAIL:
PHONE:	PHONE:

BUSINESS	BUSINESS
WEBSITE:	WEBSITE:
EMAIL:	EMAIL:
PHONE:	PHONE:

BUSINESS	BUSINESS
WEBSITE:	WEBSITE:
EMAIL:	EMAIL:
PHONE:	PHONE:

BUSINESS	BUSINESS
WEBSITE:	WEBSITE:
EMAIL:	EMAIL:
PHONE:	PHONE:

BUSINESS	BUSINESS
WEBSITE:	WEBSITE:
EMAIL:	EMAIL:
PHONE:	PHONE:

Shipping TRACKER

ORDER NUMBER:	DESCRIPTION OF ITEM:	SHIP DATE:	TRACKING #:

Returns TRACKER

ORDER DATE:	ORDER #:	ITEM DESCRIPTION:	REASON:

Monthly SALES

JANUARY	FEBRUARY	MARCH

APRIL	MAY	JUNE

Monthly SALES

JULY

AUGUST

SEPTEMBER

OCTOBER

NOVEMBER

DECEMBER

Product PLANNER

PRODUCT DESCRIPTION:

SUPPLIES NEEDED:

PRODUCTION COST BREAKDOWN & EXPENSES

SUPPLIES:

MATERIALS:

LABOR:

SHIPPING:

FEES:

OTHER:

STORAGE:

TOTAL COST:

IMPORTANT NOTES

OTHER INFORMATION

Marketing PLANNER

MONTH: ....

RESOURCES:

START: **END:**

ADVERTISING BREAKDOWN & OVERVIEW

CAMPAIGN: **BUDGET:**

AUDIENCE: **COST:**

REACH: **LEADS:**

TRAFFIC: **REBOOK:**

IMPORTANT NOTES

Monthly BUSINESS GOALS

YEAR: ....

JANUARY	FEBRUARY	MARCH

APRIL	MAY	JUNE

JULY	AUGUST	SEPTEMBER

OCTOBER	NOVEMBER	DECEMBER

NOTES:

Yearly BUSINESS GOALS

YEAR: **MAIN OBJECTIVE:**

GOAL #1:   GOAL #2:

STEPS I'LL TAKE TO ACHIEVE MY GOALS: **GOAL THIS WILL ACCOMPLISH**

Notes

$\mathcal{My}$ BUSINESS GOALS

GOAL

START DATE: DATE OF COMPLETION:

GOAL PROGRESS

GOAL

START DATE: DATE OF COMPLETION:

GOAL PROGRESS

GOAL

START DATE: DATE OF COMPLETION:

GOAL PROGRESS

GOAL

START DATE: DATE OF COMPLETION:

GOAL PROGRESS

GOAL

START DATE: DATE OF COMPLETION:

GOAL PROGRESS

GOAL

START DATE: DATE OF COMPLETION::

GOAL PROGRESS

IMPORTANT NOTES	REMINDERS

$\mathcal{My}$ BUSINESS GOALS

GOAL

PRIORITY:

START DATE: DEADLINE:

STEPS TO ACHIEVE MY GOAL:

ACTION STEPS	COMPLETE BY	NOTES

MILESTONES	MILESTONES	MILESTONES

Order FORM

DATE

ORDER #:

CUSTOMER: EMAIL: PHONE #:

MAILING ADDRESS:

ITEM#	DESCRIPTION	QTY	PRICE	CUSTOMER NOTES

OF PRODUCTS ORDERED:

TOTAL UNIT PRICE: TAX:

APPLIED DISCOUNTS: SHIPPING COST:

PAYMENT METHOD: ORDER DATE:

TOTAL COST:

Order TRACKER

DATE

ORDER #:

CUSTOMER: EMAIL: PHONE #:

PRODUCT:	QTY	SHIP DATE		PRODUCT:	QTY	SHIP DATE	
			☐				☐
			☐				☐
			☐				☐
			☐				☐
			☐				☐
			☐				☐

TRACKING NUMBER: DELIVERED

NOTES:

DATE

ORDER #:

CUSTOMER: EMAIL: PHONE #:

PRODUCT:	QTY	SHIP DATE		PRODUCT:	QTY	SHIP DATE	
			☐				☐
			☐				☐
			☐				☐
			☐				☐
			☐				☐
			☐				☐

TRACKING NUMBER: DELIVERED

NOTES:

Weekly BUSINESS GOALS

WEEK OF: ....

GOAL:

GOAL:

GOAL:

GOAL:

GOAL:

GOAL:

Business NOTES

Ideas

Notes

Monthly SALES

DATE:	SOURCE	PRICE:	PROFIT:

Monthly INCOME TRACKER

MONTH: **YEAR:**

DATE: **DESCRIPTION:**   **GROSS:**   **NET:**

Monthly EXPENSES

MONTH: _____   YEAR: _____

DATE:	DESCRIPTION:	INVOICE #:	AMOUNT:

Monthly BUDGET

MONTH: **YEAR:**

OVERVIEW:	BUDGETED:	ACTUAL COST:
INCOME:		
EXPENSES:		
SAVINGS:		
OTHER:		

EXPENSE TRACKER

SUMMARY:	BUDGETED:	ACTUAL COST:	NOTES:

Product INVENTORY

PRODUCT:	DESCRIPTION:	QTY:	COST:

Mileage TRACKER

PERIOD OF:

DATE:	TO:	FROM:	PURPOSE:	TOTAL DISTANCE

Product PRICING

ITEM:	SUPPLY COST:	LABOR:	SHIPPING COST:	PROFIT:

Tax DEDUCTIONS

MONTH: **YEAR:**

DATE: **DESCRIPTION:**   **AMOUNT:**   **NOTES:**

Discount TRACKER

MONTH: **YEAR:**

ITEM:	DESCRIPTION:	REG PRICE:	SALE PRICE:

Shipping TRACKER

ORDER #:	PRODUCT DESCRIPTION:	SHIP DATE:	TRACKING #:	SHIPPED:

Supplier CONTACTS

NAME

BUSINESS

WEBSITE:

EMAIL:

PHONE:

NAME

BUSINESS

WEBSITE:

EMAIL:

PHONE:

BUSINESS

WEBSITE:

EMAIL:

PHONE:

BUSINESS

WEBSITE:

EMAIL:

PHONE:

BUSINESS

WEBSITE:

EMAIL:

PHONE:

BUSINESS

WEBSITE:

EMAIL:

PHONE:

BUSINESS

WEBSITE:

EMAIL:

PHONE:

BUSINESS

WEBSITE:

EMAIL:

PHONE:

BUSINESS

WEBSITE:

EMAIL:

PHONE:

BUSINESS

WEBSITE:

EMAIL:

PHONE:

Shipping TRACKER

ORDER NUMBER: **DESCRIPTION OF ITEM:**   **SHIP DATE:**   **TRACKING #:**

Returns TRACKER

ORDER DATE:	ORDER #:	ITEM DESCRIPTION:	REASON:

Monthly SALES

JANUARY

FEBRUARY

MARCH

APRIL

MAY

JUNE

Monthly SALES

JULY	AUGUST	SEPTEMBER

OCTOBER	NOVEMBER	DECEMBER

Product PLANNER

PRODUCT DESCRIPTION: **SUPPLIES NEEDED:**

PRODUCTION COST BREAKDOWN & EXPENSES

SUPPLIES: **MATERIALS:**

LABOR: **SHIPPING:**

FEES: **OTHER:**

STORAGE: **TOTAL COST:**

IMPORTANT NOTES   **OTHER INFORMATION**

Marketing PLANNER

MONTH: ....

RESOURCES:

START:

END:

ADVERTISING BREAKDOWN & OVERVIEW

CAMPAIGN:

BUDGET:

AUDIENCE:

COST:

REACH:

LEADS:

TRAFFIC:

REBOOK:

IMPORTANT NOTES

Monthly BUSINESS GOALS

YEAR: ....

JANUARY

FEBRUARY

MARCH

APRIL

MAY

JUNE

JULY

AUGUST

SEPTEMBER

OCTOBER

NOVEMBER

DECEMBER

NOTES:

Yearly BUSINESS GOALS

YEAR:

MAIN OBJECTIVE:

GOAL #1:

GOAL #2:

STEPS I'LL TAKE TO ACHIEVE MY GOALS:

GOAL THIS WILL ACCOMPLISH

Notes

My BUSINESS GOALS

GOAL

START DATE: DATE OF COMPLETION:

GOAL PROGRESS

GOAL

START DATE: DATE OF COMPLETION:

GOAL PROGRESS

GOAL

START DATE: DATE OF COMPLETION:

GOAL PROGRESS

GOAL

START DATE: DATE OF COMPLETION:

GOAL PROGRESS

GOAL

START DATE: DATE OF COMPLETION:

GOAL PROGRESS

GOAL

START DATE: DATE OF COMPLETION::

GOAL PROGRESS

IMPORTANT NOTES   **REMINDERS**

My BUSINESS GOALS

GOAL

PRIORITY:

🕐 START DATE: DEADLINE:

STEPS TO ACHIEVE MY GOAL:

ACTION STEPS	COMPLETE BY	NOTES

MILESTONES   MILESTONES   MILESTONES

Order FORM

DATE

ORDER #:

CUSTOMER: EMAIL: PHONE #:

MAILING ADDRESS:

ITEM#	DESCRIPTION	QTY	PRICE	CUSTOMER NOTES

OF PRODUCTS ORDERED:

TOTAL UNIT PRICE: TAX:

APPLIED DISCOUNTS: SHIPPING COST:

PAYMENT METHOD: ORDER DATE:

TOTAL COST:

Order TRACKER

DATE

ORDER #:

CUSTOMER: EMAIL: PHONE #:

PRODUCT:	QTY	SHIP DATE		PRODUCT:	QTY	SHIP DATE
		☐				☐
		☐				☐
		☐				☐
		☐				☐
		☐				☐
		☐				☐

TRACKING NUMBER: DELIVERED

NOTES:

DATE

ORDER #:

CUSTOMER: EMAIL: PHONE #:

PRODUCT:	QTY	SHIP DATE		PRODUCT:	QTY	SHIP DATE
		☐				☐
		☐				☐
		☐				☐
		☐				☐
		☐				☐
		☐				☐

TRACKING NUMBER: DELIVERED

NOTES:

Weekly BUSINESS GOALS

WEEK OF: ....

GOAL:

GOAL:

GOAL:

GOAL:

GOAL:

GOAL:

Business NOTES

_____

_____

_____

_____

_____

_____

_____

_____

_____

_____

_____

_____

_____

_____

_____

_____

_____

_____

_____

_____

_____

_____

Ideas

Notes

Monthly SALES

DATE:	SOURCE	PRICE:	PROFIT:

Monthly INCOME TRACKER

MONTH: **YEAR:**

DATE:	DESCRIPTION:	GROSS:	NET:

Monthly EXPENSES

MONTH: **YEAR:**

DATE: **DESCRIPTION:**   **INVOICE #:**   **AMOUNT:**

Monthly BUDGET

MONTH: **YEAR:**

OVERVIEW:	BUDGETED:	ACTUAL COST:
INCOME:		
EXPENSES:		
SAVINGS:		
OTHER:		

EXPENSE TRACKER

SUMMARY:	BUDGETED:	ACTUAL COST:	NOTES:

Product INVENTORY

PRODUCT:	DESCRIPTION:	QTY:	COST:

Mileage TRACKER

PERIOD OF:

DATE:	TO:	FROM:	PURPOSE:	TOTAL DISTANCE

Product PRICING

ITEM:	SUPPLY COST:	LABOR:	SHIPPING COST:	PROFIT:

Tax DEDUCTIONS

MONTH: **YEAR:**

DATE:	DESCRIPTION:	AMOUNT:	NOTES:

Discount TRACKER

MONTH: **YEAR:**

ITEM:	DESCRIPTION:	REG PRICE:	SALE PRICE:

Shipping TRACKER

ORDER #:	PRODUCT DESCRIPTION:	SHIP DATE:	TRACKING #:	SHIPPED:

Supplier CONTACTS

NAME

BUSINESS

WEBSITE:

EMAIL:

PHONE:

NAME

BUSINESS

WEBSITE:

EMAIL:

PHONE:

BUSINESS

WEBSITE:

EMAIL:

PHONE:

BUSINESS

WEBSITE:

EMAIL:

PHONE:

BUSINESS

WEBSITE:

EMAIL:

PHONE:

BUSINESS

WEBSITE:

EMAIL:

PHONE:

BUSINESS

WEBSITE:

EMAIL:

PHONE:

BUSINESS

WEBSITE:

EMAIL:

PHONE:

BUSINESS

WEBSITE:

EMAIL:

PHONE:

BUSINESS

WEBSITE:

EMAIL:

PHONE:

Shipping TRACKER

ORDER NUMBER:	DESCRIPTION OF ITEM:	SHIP DATE:	TRACKING #:

Returns TRACKER

| ORDER DATE: | ORDER #: | ITEM DESCRIPTION: | REASON: |

Monthly SALES

JANUARY

FEBRUARY

MARCH

APRIL

MAY

JUNE

Monthly SALES

JULY   **AUGUST**   **SEPTEMBER**

OCTOBER   **NOVEMBER**   **DECEMBER**

Product PLANNER

PRODUCT DESCRIPTION:

SUPPLIES NEEDED:

PRODUCTION COST BREAKDOWN & EXPENSES

SUPPLIES:

MATERIALS:

LABOR:

SHIPPING:

FEES:

OTHER:

STORAGE:

TOTAL COST:

IMPORTANT NOTES

OTHER INFORMATION

Marketing PLANNER

MONTH: ....

RESOURCES:

START: **END:**

ADVERTISING BREAKDOWN & OVERVIEW

CAMPAIGN: **BUDGET:**

AUDIENCE: **COST:**

REACH: **LEADS:**

TRAFFIC: **REBOOK:**

IMPORTANT NOTES

Monthly BUSINESS GOALS

YEAR: ....

JANUARY	FEBRUARY	MARCH

APRIL	MAY	JUNE

JULY	AUGUST	SEPTEMBER

OCTOBER	NOVEMBER	DECEMBER

NOTES:

Yearly BUSINESS GOALS

YEAR:

MAIN OBJECTIVE:

GOAL #1:   **GOAL #2:**

STEPS I'LL TAKE TO ACHIEVE MY GOALS: **GOAL THIS WILL ACCOMPLISH**

$\mathcal{My}$ BUSINESS GOALS

GOAL

START DATE: DATE OF COMPLETION:

GOAL PROGRESS

GOAL

START DATE: DATE OF COMPLETION:

GOAL PROGRESS

GOAL

START DATE: DATE OF COMPLETION:

GOAL PROGRESS

GOAL

START DATE: DATE OF COMPLETION:

GOAL PROGRESS

GOAL

START DATE: DATE OF COMPLETION:

GOAL PROGRESS

GOAL

START DATE: DATE OF COMPLETION::

GOAL PROGRESS

IMPORTANT NOTES	**REMINDERS**

My BUSINESS GOALS

GOAL

PRIORITY:

🕐 START DATE: DEADLINE:

STEPS TO ACHIEVE MY GOAL:

ACTION STEPS   COMPLETE BY   NOTES

MILESTONES   MILESTONES   MILESTONES

Order FORM

DATE

ORDER #:

CUSTOMER: EMAIL: PHONE #:

MAILING ADDRESS:

ITEM#	DESCRIPTION	QTY	PRICE	CUSTOMER NOTES

OF PRODUCTS ORDERED:

TOTAL UNIT PRICE: TAX:

APPLIED DISCOUNTS: SHIPPING COST:

PAYMENT METHOD: ORDER DATE:

TOTAL COST:

Order TRACKER

DATE

ORDER #:

CUSTOMER: EMAIL: PHONE #:

PRODUCT:	QTY	SHIP DATE		PRODUCT:	QTY	SHIP DATE
			☐				☐
			☐				☐
			☐				☐
			☐				☐
			☐				☐
			☐				☐

TRACKING NUMBER: DELIVERED

NOTES:

DATE

ORDER #:

CUSTOMER: EMAIL: PHONE #:

PRODUCT:	QTY	SHIP DATE		PRODUCT:	QTY	SHIP DATE
			☐				☐
			☐				☐
			☐				☐
			☐				☐
			☐				☐
			☐				☐

TRACKING NUMBER: DELIVERED

NOTES:

Weekly BUSINESS GOALS

WEEK OF: ....

GOAL:

GOAL:

GOAL:

GOAL:

GOAL:

GOAL:

Business NOTES

Ideas

Notes

Monthly SALES

DATE:	SOURCE	PRICE:	PROFIT:

Monthly INCOME TRACKER

MONTH: **YEAR:**

DATE: **DESCRIPTION:**   **GROSS:**   **NET:**

Monthly EXPENSES

MONTH: _____   **YEAR:** _____

DATE:	DESCRIPTION:	INVOICE #:	AMOUNT:

Monthly BUDGET

MONTH: **YEAR:**

OVERVIEW:	BUDGETED:	ACTUAL COST:
INCOME:		
EXPENSES:		
SAVINGS:		
OTHER:		

EXPENSE TRACKER

SUMMARY:	BUDGETED:	ACTUAL COST:	NOTES:

Product INVENTORY

PRODUCT:	DESCRIPTION:	QTY:	COST:

Mileage TRACKER

PERIOD OF:

DATE:	TO:	FROM:	PURPOSE:	TOTAL DISTANCE

Product PRICING

ITEM:	SUPPLY COST:	LABOR:	SHIPPING COST:	PROFIT:

Tax DEDUCTIONS

MONTH: **YEAR:**

DATE: **DESCRIPTION:**   **AMOUNT:**   **NOTES:**

Discount TRACKER

MONTH: **YEAR:**

ITEM:	DESCRIPTION:	REG PRICE:	SALE PRICE:

Shipping TRACKER

ORDER #:	PRODUCT DESCRIPTION:	SHIP DATE:	TRACKING #:	SHIPPED:

Supplier CONTACTS

NAME

NAME

BUSINESS

BUSINESS

WEBSITE:

WEBSITE:

EMAIL:

EMAIL:

PHONE:

PHONE:

BUSINESS

BUSINESS

WEBSITE:

WEBSITE:

EMAIL:

EMAIL:

PHONE:

PHONE:

BUSINESS

BUSINESS

WEBSITE:

WEBSITE:

EMAIL:

EMAIL:

PHONE:

PHONE:

BUSINESS

BUSINESS

WEBSITE:

WEBSITE:

EMAIL:

EMAIL:

PHONE:

PHONE:

BUSINESS

BUSINESS

WEBSITE:

WEBSITE:

EMAIL:

EMAIL:

PHONE:

PHONE:

Shipping TRACKER

ORDER NUMBER:	DESCRIPTION OF ITEM:	SHIP DATE:	TRACKING #:

Returns TRACKER

ORDER DATE:	ORDER #:	ITEM DESCRIPTION:	REASON:

Monthly SALES

JANUARY

FEBRUARY

MARCH

APRIL

MAY

JUNE

Monthly SALES

JULY	AUGUST	SEPTEMBER

OCTOBER	NOVEMBER	DECEMBER

PRODUCT DESCRIPTION: **SUPPLIES NEEDED:**

PRODUCTION COST BREAKDOWN & EXPENSES

SUPPLIES: **MATERIALS:**

LABOR: **SHIPPING:**

FEES: **OTHER:**

STORAGE: **TOTAL COST:**

IMPORTANT NOTES   **OTHER INFORMATION**

Marketing PLANNER

MONTH: ....

RESOURCES:

START: **END:**

ADVERTISING BREAKDOWN & OVERVIEW

CAMPAIGN: **BUDGET:**

AUDIENCE: **COST:**

REACH: **LEADS:**

TRAFFIC: **REBOOK:**

IMPORTANT NOTES

Monthly BUSINESS GOALS

YEAR: ....

JANUARY

FEBRUARY

MARCH

APRIL

MAY

JUNE

JULY

AUGUST

SEPTEMBER

OCTOBER

NOVEMBER

DECEMBER

NOTES:

Yearly BUSINESS GOALS

YEAR:

MAIN OBJECTIVE:

GOAL #1:

GOAL #2:

STEPS I'LL TAKE TO ACHIEVE MY GOALS:

GOAL THIS WILL ACCOMPLISH

Notes

$\mathcal{My}$ BUSINESS GOALS

GOAL

START DATE: DATE OF COMPLETION:

GOAL PROGRESS

GOAL

START DATE: DATE OF COMPLETION:

GOAL PROGRESS

GOAL

START DATE: DATE OF COMPLETION:

GOAL PROGRESS

GOAL

START DATE: DATE OF COMPLETION:

GOAL PROGRESS

GOAL

START DATE: DATE OF COMPLETION:

GOAL PROGRESS

GOAL

START DATE: DATE OF COMPLETION::

GOAL PROGRESS

IMPORTANT NOTES   **REMINDERS**

My BUSINESS GOALS

GOAL

PRIORITY:

START DATE: DEADLINE:

STEPS TO ACHIEVE MY GOAL:

ACTION STEPS	COMPLETE BY	NOTES

MILESTONES   MILESTONES   MILESTONES

Order FORM

DATE

ORDER #:

CUSTOMER: EMAIL: PHONE #:

MAILING ADDRESS:

ITEM#	DESCRIPTION	QTY	PRICE	CUSTOMER NOTES

 # OF PRODUCTS ORDERED:

TOTAL UNIT PRICE: TAX:

APPLIED DISCOUNTS: SHIPPING COST:

PAYMENT METHOD: ORDER DATE:

TOTAL COST:

Order TRACKER

DATE

ORDER #:

CUSTOMER: EMAIL: PHONE #:

PRODUCT:	QTY	SHIP DATE		PRODUCT:	QTY	SHIP DATE
		☐				☐
		☐				☐
		☐				☐
		☐				☐
		☐				☐
		☐				☐

TRACKING NUMBER: DELIVERED

NOTES:

DATE

ORDER #:

CUSTOMER: EMAIL: PHONE #:

PRODUCT:	QTY	SHIP DATE		PRODUCT:	QTY	SHIP DATE
		☐				☐
		☐				☐
		☐				☐
		☐				☐
		☐				☐
		☐				☐

TRACKING NUMBER: DELIVERED

NOTES:

Weekly BUSINESS GOALS

WEEK OF: ....

GOAL:

GOAL:

GOAL:

GOAL:

GOAL:

GOAL:

Business NOTES

_____

Ideas

Notes

Monthly SALES

DATE: **SOURCE**   **PRICE:**   **PROFIT:**

Monthly INCOME TRACKER

MONTH: **YEAR:**

DATE:	DESCRIPTION:	GROSS:	NET:

Monthly EXPENSES

MONTH: **YEAR:**

DATE: **DESCRIPTION:**   **INVOICE #:**   **AMOUNT:**

Monthly BUDGET

MONTH: **YEAR:**

OVERVIEW:	BUDGETED:	ACTUAL COST:
INCOME:		
EXPENSES:		
SAVINGS:		
OTHER:		

EXPENSE TRACKER

SUMMARY:	BUDGETED:	ACTUAL COST:	NOTES:

Product INVENTORY

PRODUCT:	DESCRIPTION:	QTY:	COST:

Mileage TRACKER

PERIOD OF:

DATE:	TO:	FROM:	PURPOSE:	TOTAL DISTANCE

Product PRICING

ITEM:	SUPPLY COST:	LABOR:	SHIPPING COST:	PROFIT:

Tax DEDUCTIONS

MONTH: _____   YEAR: _____

DATE:	DESCRIPTION:	AMOUNT:	NOTES:

Discount TRACKER

MONTH: **YEAR:**

ITEM: **DESCRIPTION:**   **REG PRICE:**   **SALE PRICE:**

Shipping TRACKER

ORDER #:	PRODUCT DESCRIPTION:	SHIP DATE:	TRACKING #:	SHIPPED:

Supplier CONTACTS

NAME	NAME
BUSINESS	BUSINESS
WEBSITE:	WEBSITE:
EMAIL:	EMAIL:
PHONE:	PHONE:

BUSINESS	BUSINESS
WEBSITE:	WEBSITE:
EMAIL:	EMAIL:
PHONE:	PHONE:

BUSINESS	BUSINESS
WEBSITE:	WEBSITE:
EMAIL:	EMAIL:
PHONE:	PHONE:

BUSINESS	BUSINESS
WEBSITE:	WEBSITE:
EMAIL:	EMAIL:
PHONE:	PHONE:

BUSINESS	BUSINESS
WEBSITE:	WEBSITE:
EMAIL:	EMAIL:
PHONE:	PHONE:

Shipping TRACKER

ORDER NUMBER:	DESCRIPTION OF ITEM:	SHIP DATE:	TRACKING #:

Returns TRACKER

ORDER DATE:	ORDER #:	ITEM DESCRIPTION:	REASON:

Monthly SALES

JANUARY	FEBRUARY	MARCH

APRIL	MAY	JUNE

Monthly SALES

JULY   **AUGUST**   **SEPTEMBER**

OCTOBER   **NOVEMBER**   **DECEMBER**

Product PLANNER

PRODUCT DESCRIPTION:

SUPPLIES NEEDED:

PRODUCTION COST BREAKDOWN & EXPENSES

SUPPLIES:

MATERIALS:

LABOR:

SHIPPING:

FEES:

OTHER:

STORAGE:

TOTAL COST:

IMPORTANT NOTES

OTHER INFORMATION

Marketing PLANNER

MONTH: ....

RESOURCES:

START: **END:**

ADVERTISING BREAKDOWN & OVERVIEW

CAMPAIGN: **BUDGET:**

AUDIENCE: **COST:**

REACH: **LEADS:**

TRAFFIC: **REBOOK:**

IMPORTANT NOTES

Monthly BUSINESS GOALS

YEAR: ....

JANUARY	FEBRUARY	MARCH

APRIL	MAY	JUNE

JULY	AUGUST	SEPTEMBER

OCTOBER	NOVEMBER	DECEMBER

NOTES:

Yearly BUSINESS GOALS

YEAR:

MAIN OBJECTIVE:

GOAL #1:

GOAL #2:

STEPS I'LL TAKE TO ACHIEVE MY GOALS:

GOAL THIS WILL ACCOMPLISH

$\mathcal{My}$ BUSINESS GOALS

GOAL

START DATE: DATE OF COMPLETION:

GOAL PROGRESS

GOAL

START DATE: DATE OF COMPLETION:

GOAL PROGRESS

GOAL

START DATE: DATE OF COMPLETION:

GOAL PROGRESS

GOAL

START DATE: DATE OF COMPLETION:

GOAL PROGRESS

GOAL

START DATE: DATE OF COMPLETION:

GOAL PROGRESS

GOAL

START DATE: DATE OF COMPLETION::

GOAL PROGRESS

IMPORTANT NOTES   **REMINDERS**

My BUSINESS GOALS

GOAL

PRIORITY:

START DATE: DEADLINE:

STEPS TO ACHIEVE MY GOAL:

ACTION STEPS	COMPLETE BY	NOTES

MILESTONES   MILESTONES   MILESTONES

Order FORM

ORDER #:

CUSTOMER: EMAIL: PHONE #:

MAILING ADDRESS:

ITEM#	DESCRIPTION	QTY	PRICE	CUSTOMER NOTES

OF PRODUCTS ORDERED:

TOTAL UNIT PRICE: TAX:

APPLIED DISCOUNTS: SHIPPING COST:

PAYMENT METHOD: ORDER DATE:

TOTAL COST:

Order TRACKER

DATE

ORDER #:

CUSTOMER: EMAIL: PHONE #:

PRODUCT:	QTY	SHIP DATE		PRODUCT:	QTY	SHIP DATE	
			☐				☐
			☐				☐
			☐				☐
			☐				☐
			☐				☐
			☐				☐

TRACKING NUMBER: DELIVERED

NOTES:

DATE

ORDER #:

CUSTOMER: EMAIL: PHONE #:

PRODUCT:	QTY	SHIP DATE		PRODUCT:	QTY	SHIP DATE	
			☐				☐
			☐				☐
			☐				☐
			☐				☐
			☐				☐
			☐				☐

TRACKING NUMBER: DELIVERED

NOTES:

Weekly BUSINESS GOALS

WEEK OF: ....

GOAL:

GOAL:

GOAL:

GOAL:

GOAL:

GOAL:

Business NOTES

Ideas

Notes

Monthly SALES

DATE:	SOURCE	PRICE:	PROFIT:

Monthly INCOME TRACKER

MONTH: **YEAR:**

DATE: **DESCRIPTION:**   **GROSS:**   **NET:**

Monthly EXPENSES

MONTH: **YEAR:**

DATE:	DESCRIPTION:	INVOICE #:	AMOUNT:

Monthly BUDGET

MONTH: **YEAR:**

OVERVIEW:	BUDGETED:	ACTUAL COST:
INCOME:		
EXPENSES:		
SAVINGS:		
OTHER:		

EXPENSE TRACKER

SUMMARY:	BUDGETED:	ACTUAL COST:	NOTES:

Product INVENTORY

PRODUCT:	DESCRIPTION:	QTY:	COST:

Mileage TRACKER

PERIOD OF:

DATE: **TO:**   **FROM:**   **PURPOSE:**   **TOTAL DISTANCE**

Product PRICING

ITEM:	SUPPLY COST:	LABOR:	SHIPPING COST:	PROFIT:

Tax DEDUCTIONS

MONTH: **YEAR:**

DATE: **DESCRIPTION:**   **AMOUNT:**   **NOTES:**

Discount TRACKER

MONTH: **YEAR:**

ITEM:	DESCRIPTION:	REG PRICE:	SALE PRICE:

Shipping TRACKER

ORDER #:	PRODUCT DESCRIPTION:	SHIP DATE:	TRACKING #:	SHIPPED:

Supplier CONTACTS

NAME	NAME
BUSINESS	BUSINESS
WEBSITE:	WEBSITE:
EMAIL:	EMAIL:
PHONE:	PHONE:

BUSINESS	BUSINESS
WEBSITE:	WEBSITE:
EMAIL:	EMAIL:
PHONE:	PHONE:

BUSINESS	BUSINESS
WEBSITE:	WEBSITE:
EMAIL:	EMAIL:
PHONE:	PHONE:

BUSINESS	BUSINESS
WEBSITE:	WEBSITE:
EMAIL:	EMAIL:
PHONE:	PHONE:

BUSINESS	BUSINESS
WEBSITE:	WEBSITE:
EMAIL:	EMAIL:
PHONE:	PHONE:

Shipping TRACKER

ORDER NUMBER:	DESCRIPTION OF ITEM:	SHIP DATE:	TRACKING #:

Returns TRACKER

ORDER DATE:	ORDER #:	ITEM DESCRIPTION:	REASON:

Monthly SALES

JANUARY

FEBRUARY

MARCH

APRIL

MAY

JUNE

 Monthly SALES

JULY	AUGUST	SEPTEMBER

OCTOBER	NOVEMBER	DECEMBER

Product PLANNER

PRODUCT DESCRIPTION: **SUPPLIES NEEDED:**

PRODUCTION COST BREAKDOWN & EXPENSES

SUPPLIES: **MATERIALS:**

LABOR: **SHIPPING:**

FEES: **OTHER:**

STORAGE: **TOTAL COST:**

IMPORTANT NOTES   **OTHER INFORMATION**

Marketing PLANNER

MONTH: ....

RESOURCES:

START: **END:**

ADVERTISING BREAKDOWN & OVERVIEW

CAMPAIGN: **BUDGET:**

AUDIENCE: **COST:**

REACH: **LEADS:**

TRAFFIC: **REBOOK:**

IMPORTANT NOTES

Monthly BUSINESS GOALS

YEAR: ....

JANUARY   **FEBRUARY**   **MARCH**

APRIL   **MAY**   **JUNE**

JULY   **AUGUST**   **SEPTEMBER**

OCTOBER   **NOVEMBER**   **DECEMBER**

NOTES:

Yearly BUSINESS GOALS

YEAR:

MAIN OBJECTIVE:

GOAL #1:

GOAL #2:

STEPS I'LL TAKE TO ACHIEVE MY GOALS:

GOAL THIS WILL ACCOMPLISH

Notes

My BUSINESS GOALS

GOAL

START DATE: DATE OF COMPLETION:

GOAL PROGRESS

GOAL

START DATE: DATE OF COMPLETION:

GOAL PROGRESS

GOAL

START DATE: DATE OF COMPLETION:

GOAL PROGRESS

GOAL

START DATE: DATE OF COMPLETION:

GOAL PROGRESS

GOAL

START DATE: DATE OF COMPLETION:

GOAL PROGRESS

GOAL

START DATE: DATE OF COMPLETION::

GOAL PROGRESS

IMPORTANT NOTES   **REMINDERS**

My BUSINESS GOALS

GOAL

PRIORITY:

🕐 START DATE: DEADLINE:

STEPS TO ACHIEVE MY GOAL:

ACTION STEPS	COMPLETE BY	NOTES

MILESTONES   MILESTONES   MILESTONES

Made in the USA
Coppell, TX
14 December 2021

68496792R00083